COPTIC GOSPEL OF THE TWELVE APOSTLES

Translated by: Eugene Revillout, D.P. Curtin

Copyright @ 2020 Dalcassian Press

All rights reserved. No part of this publication may be reproduced, distributed, or transmitted in any form or by any means, including photocopying, recording, or other electronic or mechanical methods, without the prior written permission of the publisher, except in the case of brief quotations embodied in critical reviews and certain other non-commercial uses permitted by copyright law. For permission request, write to Dalcassian Press at dalcassianpublishing at gmail.com

ISBN: 979-8-3302-6688-3 (Paperback)

Library of Congress Control Number:
Author: Curtin, D.P. (1985-)

Printed by Ingram Content Group, 1 Ingram Blvd, La Vergne, Tennessee

First printing edition 2020.

COPTIC GOSPEL OF THE TWELVE APOSTLES
Based upon the French translation by: Eugene Revillout

1st FRAGMENT

(Herod), too, was tetrarch over Galilee. Finally, Satan entered into him. He rose. He went to the Emperor Tiberius. He accused Philip before him, saying: [...]

[This emperor] became very angry, saying, "So now the whole world is subject to my power since the time when God gave these things into the hands of my father Augustus. And Philip will incite seditions against my kingship and my great power. I will not allow it." And he ordered, [...]

"You shall confiscate Philip, take away his house. You shall seize his servants, his livestock, all his riches, everything that belongs to him and you will send me these things to the seat of my empire. All his possessions, you will count for me, and you will leave him nothing, except his life, that of his wife, and (that of his daughter)."

[Here is what Tiberius said] to the impious Herod.

He went, along with those who were sent with him. He took Philip without him knowing anything and without him knowing the matter [for which he was being treated like this].

2nd FRAGMENT

[...] "My friends. Have you seen, O my brothers, a Lord like this one, loving his apostles, promising them his kingdom so that they may eat and drink with him at the table of his kingdom? Since He was on earth, He ate with them at the table of the earth, reminding them of the table of his kingdom; for he considered the things of the world as nothing."

"If you want to know, listen, and I will teach you. Did God not love his apostles, all of them? Listen to John the Evangelist testifying that Christ."

He prayed to his Father for them, "that they may be one, as we are one." You want to know the truth, for he chose the twelve so that they would be as such. Then he said, "I have compassion for this crowd, because behold, they have been with me for three days and have nothing to eat. I do not want to send them away hungry, lest they faint on the way."

Andrew said to him, "Lord, where will we find bread in this desolate place, for [...]"

Jesus said to Thomas, "Go to this man. He has five barley loaves in his hand and two fish. Bring them to me here."

Andrew said, "Master, what will these five loaves do for such a large crowd?"

Jesus said to him, "Bring them to me and that will be enough."

They went. They brought the little child to Jesus and he worshiped Him immediately. He brought him the loaves and the two fish.

The child said to Jesus: "Master, I have taken much trouble for these."

Jesus said to the child: "Give me the five loaves you are the guardian of. Because it is not you who saves this multitude from need, but it is a providential plan so that you may see an admirable thing whose memory will never disappear and a food with which they will be satisfied."

Jesus took the bread. He gave thanks for it. He divided it. He gave it to his apostles to bring to the multitude. Judas was the last one to partake of the bread. Andrew said to Jesus: "Master, Judas did not receive a share of the bread when he came to give it to the multitude; and you wanted us to give [...]"

(Jesus said:) "It is your word; for whoever I have not shared the bread from my hands with is not worthy of sharing my flesh. And besides, he does not care about giving to the poor, but only cares about the money bag. It is a mystery of my Father concerning the sharing of my flesh."

Then he blessed them saying: "My Father, source of all goodness, I pray that you bless these five barley loaves so that they may satisfy this whole multitude, so that your son may receive glory in you and that those whom you have drawn to him out of the world may obey him."

Then his word became powerful. His blessing entered the bread and among the apostles. And the entire people ate and were satisfied. They blessed God.

You have seen, O beloved, the love of Jesus for his apostles; for he did not hide anything from them in the works of his divinity once in the blessing of the five barley loaves; once in the thanksgiving to his Father; once in giving thanks for the seven loaves.

Thomas said to Jesus, "My Lord, behold, all the grace you have done with us in your goodness. There is one thing that we want you to grant us: we want, my Lord, to see the dead resting in the tombs that you have resurrected as a sign of your resurrection that will take place for us. We know, Lord, that you resurrected the son of the widow of Nain. But another thing is the miracle of that moment, for you found them walking with him (the dead) on the way. We want to see bones that have separated in the tomb, how they will come together, so that the (dead) can speak."

Jesus said to Thomas: "Thomas, my friend, ask me, as well as your brothers, about all things that you desire. I will not hide anything from you, so that you may see, touch, and your heart may be strengthened. If you desire to see people in the tomb being resurrected, it is right that you seek a sign of the resurrection, for I have answered you saying: 'I am the resurrection and the life'. If the grain of wheat does not die, it does not bear fruit. If you also do not see with your eyes, your heart is not strengthened. Did I not tell you: 'Blessed are those who have not seen and yet believe, more than those who have seen and do not believe'. You see how many miracles and wonders I have performed before the Jews and they did not believe in me. Now, my brothers, you know Lazarus, the man from Bethany who is called my friend. It has been four days since I have been with you and I have not gone to inquire about his sisters; for it has been four days since Lazarus died. Let us go to him to comfort his sisters because of their brother Lazarus. Thomas, come with me. Let us go to Bethany. I will show you the type of resurrection on the last day in his tomb, so that your heart may be strengthened; for I am the resurrection and the life. Come with me, Thomas; I will show you the bones that were disjointed in the tomb coming back together. Come with me, Thomas; I will show you Lazarus's eyes that were hollowed out by the decay and left the light. Come with me, Didymas, to the mountain of Bethany; I will show you Lazarus's tongue that has been liquefied by the corruption and will speak with you again. Come with me, Thomas, to the tomb of Lazarus, so that you may see the destruction of the bones and his burial (his buried body) that the worms have eaten and what happens to his voice when I call him. Come with me, Didymus, to the tomb of Lazarus, even though he has been dead for four days, and I will raise him up alive again. You seek a sign of resurrection, Thomas; come and I will show it to you in the tomb of Lazarus; you seek to see bones rejoining together again; come with me to the tomb of Lazarus to see them coming and going at the door of his tomb. You seek outstretched hands; come, I will show you the hands of Lazarus bound with their bands, wrapped in shrouds, which will rise up there, coming out of the tomb. Didymus, my friend, come with me to the tomb of Lazarus; for my mouth desires what you have thought. Today is the fourth day for Lazarus. Martha and Mary are waiting for me to visit them because of their brother."

These are the things that Jesus said to his Apostles. Didymus gathered his courage. He said to him, "Lord, how shall we go there, when the Jews seek to stone you?"

He said this because he was distressed by the words that Jesus had spoken about Lazarus and did not want to go there.

Jesus said to him, "Thomas, the one who walks in the light will not stumble." Jesus spoke these words to Thomas to console him, because he saw that he was distressed about the death of Lazarus.

After all this, as they were approaching the entrance of Lazarus' tomb, his sister came to meet him there. She said to him, "Lord, if you had been here, my brother would not have died, for you are the resurrection, raising the dead. I have known you since your childhood, as well as my brother Lazarus."

Jesus said to her, "Do you believe this, that I am the resurrection, raising the dead and giving life to all?"

Martha said to him, "Yes, Lord, I believe."

Jesus said to her, "Your brother will rise again."

They said these things, Martha and Mary being with Jesus. They came to Lazarus' tomb, with Jesus walking ahead of the Apostles. He said to them, "Remove the stone from there, so that you, Thomas, may see the testimony similar to the resurrection of the dead."

At that moment, Thomas wept before Jesus, saying, "You have endured this 'weariness,' you have come to the tomb of a dead man because of my unbelief. May your will be done on me, and may this tomb receive me until the day of your resurrection."

Jesus knew that Thomas was distressed. He said to him, with a joyful voice and words of life, "Thomas, do not be distressed. You do not know what I am doing. Is it a burden to remove a stone from there for a friend who is locked in the tomb so that he may rise and come out? Do not be distressed, O Thomas. I have told you, remove the stone from there so that a testimony of resurrection may appear in a tomb of death. Do not be distressed, O Thomas. I have told you: remove the stone from there to raise the dead. Open the door of the tomb, and I will bring out the one who is dead. Remove the stone from there so that I may give life to the one who sleeps in this tomb. Take away the stone, Thomas, so that the one who is dead may find the way to come out of the tomb. If I ask you, Thomas, to remove the stone, it is not because I do not have the power to bring Lazarus out, even though the stone seals (the tomb). Yes, I have power over all things. But if you remove the stone, O Thomas, the tomb will be revealed so that all men will see it and see the dead as he sleeps. And when you remove the stone, O Thomas, is it so that the bad odor will come out and that the decay and worms appear, as happens to all the dead? No! God forbid!"

After this, Jesus said to Mary: "Do you believe that your brother will rise again?"

She said: "Yes, Lord, I believe. He already smells bad; for he has been dead four days. But I believe that you can do anything."

Jesus turned to Thomas and said to him: "Come and see the bones of the dead that lie in the tomb before I raise them. Come with me, O Thomas, and see the eyes that have liquefied before I restore them to light. Come with me, O Thomas, and see the one who sleeps, how he is placed, before I make him rise again. Come, Thomas, have faith in yourself towards me and believe that I have power over all things. Martha and Mary, strengthen your hearts, and you (Thomas), have faith in yourself more than Martha and Mary who testified to me saying: 'Yes, you have power over all things'."
Jesus said this; then he cried out, saying: "My Father, my Father, root of all goodness, I pray to you, for the time has come to give glory to your Son, so that all may know that it is you who sent me for this. Glory to you forever! Amen."

After Jesus had said these things, he cried out, saying, "Lazarus, come out!" At that moment the mountain turned like a wheel. The dead rose again and came out because of the voice of Jesus who had called out: "Lazarus, come out." At that moment, Lazarus came out, wrapped in bandages and with his face covered in a shroud. His head was tied with kuria. Jesus said, "Unbind him and let him go."

When Lazarus saw Jesus standing in front of the door of his tomb, he prostrated himself, he worshiped him. He cried out, saying, "Blessed be you, Jesus, at whose voice the Amenti trembles (the Egyptian hell, abode of the dead) and who called me, you whom all those in the Amenti desire to see the light of your divinity; blessed be you, whose voice is resurrection, because you are the one who will judge the whole world."

This is what Lazarus said to Jesus and the multitude ran to see him.

Jesus saw that the crowd was pushing to see him, as well as Lazarus. Some belonging to his race (his people) embraced him. Some visited him. His two sisters kissed his mouth. Finally, there were loud cries in the mountain of Bethany. Some shouted for joy. Some confessed, saying, "There has never been a man like this man in Israel." Others said, "We believe in the resurrection in what we saw in Lazarus' tomb today." They gathered around Lazarus, like bees on a honeycomb, because of the miracle that had taken place. Finally, Lazarus did not let go of Jesus' feet, embracing them and testifying to the crowd, saying, "The resurrection of the living and the dead is Jesus. What is the theory (the sacred procession) of this place compared to the theory of Amenti when he called my name at the door of my."

He said, "Lazarus, come forth?" I say, at that moment my father Adam recognized his voice, as if he were at the door of Amenti calling me. He spent a moment with his ear inclined towards the voice, thinking it was calling him. And Adam bore witness in these words: "The voice that I heard is that of my creator. The voice that I heard is that of my guarantor. This voice is that of the one who was my glory when he called me in paradise. Where is the moment when he used to come into paradise to call me? Who is the good son that my creator calls by name saying: 'Lazarus, come forth'? I beg you, my son Lazarus, to whom the mercy of the Almighty has come down, go forth. Convey my greetings to my Creator, oh my son Lazarus. Ah! In what time will I, too, hear this voice of life calling me." These were the things that Lazarus said to the multitude, while he was prostrate at the feet of Jesus.

The noise reached the Jewish elders, saying, "Jesus performed this miracle on the Sabbath day." They came to see Lazarus and to stone Jesus.

It so happened that during those days when Jesus raised Lazarus, a Galilean nobleman had come to see Herod regarding the administration of the regions of Philip, whom they accused before the emperor of having devastated them, under the pretext of his wife whom Herod had taken from him.

Therefore, Carios (Caius), the emperor's nobleman, when he heard of the miracles Jesus performed, hurried to go to him and saw him. Then

Carios brought news of Jesus. He said to Herod, "This man is worthy to be made king over all Judea and all the regions of Philip."

When Herod heard these things about Jesus, that he was worthy to be made king, he was greatly troubled and made serious accusations against Jesus, saying, "We do not want him to be king over Judea."

He also gathered all the Jewish elders. He told them what Carios thought about him and gave greetings from Emperor Tiberius! If any harm comes to Joseph and Nicodemus, the sword of the emperor will make you all perish and your city will be burned. When these things had happened, Herod asked each of the Jewish leaders for a pound of gold. He gathered a large sum and gave it to Carios so that news of Jesus would not reach Emperor Tiberius. Carios received the money from Herod and did not report the matter to Caesar. Joseph, seeing that the Jews were pursuing him, left Jerusalem and went to Arimathea. As for Carios, he sent the apostle John to the emperor, who told him everything about Jesus. Emperor Tiberius honored John greatly and wrote about Jesus, stating that he was to be made king, as written in the Gospels: "Our Lord Jesus, when he knew they were coming to seize him and make him king, withdrew to a solitary place." When his days of seclusion were over, he called the Apostles and said to them, "My brothers, the days of my departure from this world are near. I have granted you the same ones my Father granted me. I have not left you without teaching you all the things you desire."

"You, Peter, will rule the crowd (ros?) of your brothers. Come near me on this rock, that I may bless you and make you famous (celebrated?) throughout the whole world. Your head will not cause you torment, your eyes will not be separated from the light in sleep. Your nail will not be taken away from you. Your hair will not go away. The decay of the tomb will not destroy your body forever. The itch of your flesh will not return to your flesh forever. Bow your head, O Peter. The right hand of my Father is raised over you to ordain you as archbishop. May the twenty-four elders fill their phials with perfumes and pour them on your head, O Peter, to ordain you as archbishop. May the four animals bless me and my father and say the trisagios; for today my chosen one Peter will be ordained as archbishop. O you four eons of light, open up, for the power of my father will come into you to dwell in the mouth of my chosen one Peter. Heavenly treasures and abodes of my kingdom, rejoice today; for your keys will be given to my chosen one Peter. Powers and Dominions of heaven, rejoice; for I have given a power that will not pass away to Peter's tongue. Thrones and lordships, rejoice today; for I will give a fatherhood to my chosen one Peter over (with) thousands of peoples forever. The whole earth may rejoice, for I have given the power to loose to a merciful man and to untie. Paradise, rejoice today and spread your perfumes, for I will clothe Peter with a spotless stole forever! Amenti (hell), you mourn today as well as your powers; for I have promised Peter an eternal covenant, because I will build my Church on him and the gates of hell shall not prevail against it."

These things Jesus said while Peter was on the mountain. He said: "Simon Peter, tell me: Who am I?" And at that moment Peter looked up to the sky. He saw the seven heavens open. He saw the glory of the Father and the heavenly armies descending to earth because of his ordination. And he saw the right hand of the Father coming upon his head in a single appearance (or a single resemblance?) with the Son, both of them clothing him with the Holy Spirit, and when he alone had contemplated it, at that moment, he cried out, fell to the ground saying: "You are the Christ, the Son of the living God." Jesus said to him, "You are blessed, Simon bar Jona, for flesh and blood have not revealed these things to you. Now therefore, step aside so that I may give the power of my tongue to your tongue to bind and loose."

Then he placed his hand on his head and all the heavenly armies spoke the trisagios so that the aeons who were on the mountain cried out with them: "Holy, holy, holy high priest Peter!" When Peter received this great honor, his face shone. He shone like the sun before the apostles, like a Moses of this time. Jesus, when he saw the apostles with humble hearts within them.

3rd FRAGMENT

[...] on Peter's head. He blessed him, the Father- saying: "You shall be in the heights of my kingdom. You shall be very exalted at the right hand of my Son. Whoever you raise your hand against on earth, I, my Son, and the Holy Spirit will raise our hand against him. What you loose on earth, we will loose in heaven, and what you bind, we will bind. No one will be as exalted as you and your seat, and whoever does not participate in your seat (or who is not in communion with you), his hand will be rejected and not accepted. Your breath (spirit) will come from the breath (spirit) of my Son and the Holy Spirit, so that every man you baptize and upon whose face you breathe (through confirmation) will receive the Holy Spirit in the name of the Father, the Son, and the Holy Spirit." The cherubim, the seraphim, and all the angels replied: "Amen."

And he blessed Andrew, saying: "You will be a pillar of light in my kingdom, Jerusalem, my beloved city. Amen."

"O James, in every city you enter, you will see me and my Son before you preach there. Amen."

"You, my beloved John, the bond that is bound on the heart of my Son, your spirit and my Son's and mine, there is no separation between them. But you will be blessed in the kingdom. Amen."

"You, Philip, in every city you enter to preach the word of my Son, his cross will walk with you until they believe in you. Amen."

"You, my chosen Thomas, your faith will be an eagle of light that will fly in all lands until they believe in the name of my Son through you. Amen."

"O Bartholomew, your soul will be the dwelling place of the mysteries of my Son. Amen."

4th FRAGMENT

"Nothing can be impossible for you in the very transport of mountains. Now have faith in the love of my Father, for the perfection of all things is faith."

All these things, the Savior said to the apostles to console them on the mountain; for he knew what was being spread about him in Judea by the powers that had come to take him away to make him king. The messengers of Theophilus came to Jesus. They warned him, saying that they were looking for him, wanting to make him king. The apostles said to Jesus, "Our Lord, it is a joy for us that you be made king." Jesus said to them, "Have I not often told you that my kingdom is not of this world? Do not put joy in your heart for the kingdom of this world, oh brothers the apostles! Is it not for a time? Have I established this with you, oh my holy members and my brothers to eat with you at the table of a kingdom of this world? My kingdom remains eternally in heaven and on earth."

These things and others, Jesus said to his disciples, hidden on the mountain because they were seeking to make him king. And the authorities of Tiberius, with Pilate also exerted power a second time concerning Jesus to make him king. Pilate greatly approved them by saying: "Truly, based on the miracles and wonders that this man performs, he deserves to be made king over all Judea and its surrounding regions; based on the things I have heard about this man, he is good and worthy of being made king." This is what Pilate said before the authorities of Emperor Tiberius. Herod could not bear this without despising Pilate. He said: "You are a Galilean from Pontus, a foreigner, Egyptian. You know nothing of the law. Besides, you have not been presemt in this city long enough to know the works of this man." Herod said to him: "Whoever goes against the king's orders angers the king. No! It does not suit me for Jesus to be king over Judea." And so there was enmity between Herod and Pilate concerning Jesus from that moment. This word spread and became famous throughout Judea: "Jesus, king of the Jews." And that is why Pilate wrote the report (anadopa) about Jesus and placed this inscription on the cross: "This is Jesus, the king of the Jews."

When Herod heard these things, he became even more fixed in his madness against Jesus, saying, "My father died in hatred of Jesus from his childhood. As for me, I will not let myself die while he is alive." He gave much wealth to the authorities and sent them to the emperor, and he organized a perfidious conspiracy throughout all of Judea.

Our Lord Jesus knew everything that was being prepared against him. He said to his disciples: "The devil has prepared a chalice of deceit to have me crucified. Now, therefore, put all my mysteries in your ears. I have not left you lacking anything in the mysteries of my kingdom. I have given you all power in heaven and on earth. I have given you strength and authority over the serpents and scorpions, which are under your control. Now, rise up. Let us leave this place; for Herod is seeking me to have me killed."

Our Lord Jesus descended from the mountain with his disciples. Behold, the devil appeared before them in the form of a fisherman. Many demons followed him carrying a multitude of nets, traps, hooks, and snares, casting the nets and hooks on the mountain. The apostles, when they saw them casting their nets on all sides, and their hooks as well, were greatly astonished. They said, "Our Lord, who is this man who does these things in this desert?"

Jesus said to them, "Peter, this is the one I told you about. Satan is asking for you to sift you like wheat; but I have prayed for you, that your faith may not fail." John said to him, "What do they find in this desert?" Jesus said to him, "My beloved John, the one they are looking for, he has taken. He is the fisherman who catches all the bad fish. He is the hunter who catches all the unclean animals and anyone who is bad."

Philip said to him, "Who then has been caught by his hook, or in his nets?"

Jesus said to him, "There is a multitude that is caught by his hook or in his net."

Andrew said to him, "My Lord, what benefit does he have in causing men to sin?"

Jesus said, "Did I not come to bring to my kingdom those who are mine? He also seeks those who are his for his torment. I endured this great humiliation. I came down to the world to snatch my sheep from the death that is his."

John said to him: "to see what he does. My Lord, command me, and I will pursue him."

Jesus said, "Go, my beloved John, for I have purified you from your mother's womb."

Saint John walked toward the devil. The devil said to him, "What are you doing with these nets and what are you catching in this place?"

The devil said to him, "I have heard about you and your brothers that you are fishermen catching fish. I have come here to see your skills today. Here I am, with my servants and my nets. Also call your brothers. Let them come to this place with their nets, and let us cast them here. Whoever catches fish here, he is the master. It is not surprising to catch fish in the waters, but in this desert, it is surprising to catch fish."

John said to him, "I have finished hearing about your skills. Before I come near you in this place, cast your nets. We will see what you will catch."

At that moment, he cast them and caught all kinds of fish that were in the waters. Some were caught by their eyes, others were caught by their lips. Jesus and the apostles were watching from afar. He said to them, "See how Satan catches sinners by their limbs."

Jesus said to John, "Tell him to cast [...]"

5th FRAGMENT

We found this man stealing from the things that were thrown into the purse every day, bringing them to his wife, and depriving the poor in his service. Sometimes, when he returned home with sums in his hands, she used to rejoice in what he had done. We even saw him not taking anything for her at home according to the malice of her eyes and her insatiability. And then, she used to ridicule him.

Thus, due to the insatiability and evil eye of this woman, he remained that day and she advised him this great and terrible thing, namely: "Behold, the Jews are pursuing your Master. So get up and deliver him to them. You will be given many riches, and we will keep them in our house to live on." He rose, the unfortunate one, after listening to his wife, until he led his soul to the tartarus of Amenti, in the same way that Adam listened to his wife, until he became estranged from the glory of Paradise, so that death ruled over him and his race. Likewise, Judas listened to his wife and so he became a stranger to the things of heaven and the things of the earth to reach Amenti, the place of tears and lamentations. He went to the Jews and agreed with them for thirty pieces of silver to deliver his Lord. They gave them to him.

Thus, was fulfilled the word that was written: "they have received thirty pieces of silver for the price of the precious one."

He got up. He brought them to his evil wife. He told her.

6th FRAGMENT

The Savior put him (Mathias) with the twelve apostles and the table was before him. When the Savior reached out his hand for the food, the table would turn, so that they all reached out their hands for what the Savior was eating and he blessed it. Mathias placed a dish on which was a rooster. The salt was on the table. The Savior reached out his hand to take the salt first, and, on the rotating table, all the apostles took it.

Mathias said to Jesus: "Rabbi, you see this rooster. When the Jews saw me killing it, they said, 'We will kill your master like this rooster.'" Jesus smiled. He said, "O Mathias, the word they spoke, they will fulfill it. This rooster will crow before the dawn. It is a sign of John the Baptist who foretold before me. I am the true light that has nothing dark within it. When this rooster died, they said of me that I would die, too, whom Mary bore in her womb. I dwelt there with the Cherubim and the Seraphim. I came forth from the heaven of heavens to the earth. It was difficult for the earth to bear my glory. I became man for you. Now, therefore, this rooster will rise again." Jesus touched the rooster and said to it: "I tell you, O rooster, to live, as you have done. Let wings grow for you and let you fly in the air, to warn of the day when I will be delivered up." The rooster rose up from the dish. It flew away. Jesus said to Mathias: "Behold, the bird that you slaughtered three hours ago has risen. They will crucify me; and my blood will be the salvation of the nations; (and I will rise again on the third day) [...]"

7th FRAGMENT

"My true son, the tree in my garden, will be known beside that of the Stranger. He will be recognized by his fruit; for it is preferable to a multitude of those of the enemy(?). Truly, give me your strength, to my Father. Establish it for the one who will suffer with me for the good. Truly, I have received for myself the crown of the kingdom, the crown of those who share contempt in their humiliation and have not found rest. I am king by you, O my Father. You will make this enemy (the devil) be subject to me. Truly, this enemy will be broken by whom? By the Christ (or the gentle per on peric). Truly, the sting of death will be destroyed by whom? By the Only Son. Truly, the kingdom belongs to whom? It belongs to the Son. Truly, all things have been made by whom? By the firstborn[...]"

When he had finished this prayer to his Father, he turned to us.

She said to us: "The time has come when I will be taken from you. The spirit is willing but the flesh is weak. Stay and pray with me."

We, the apostles, wept and said to him: "Have mercy on us, O Son of God! What will be our fate?"

He answered and said to us: "Do not fear dissolution [...] But even more, do not fear power. Remember all that I have told you; for just as they persecuted me, they will also persecute you; so rejoice, for I have overcome the world."

8th FRAGMENT

"I have revealed to you all my glory and taught you all your strength as well as the mystery of your apostolate."

Truly, he had revealed these things to us and previously I have given you the testimonies concerning the teachings and blessings that he had given us on the mountain.

9th FRAGMENT

Our eyes penetrated every link. We contemplated the glory of his divinity, as well as all the glory of our lordship. He clothed us with strength for our apostolate [...] All these things became clear to us like the sun and illuminated.

10th FRAGMENT

[...] until Jesus who was in the praetorium. He said to him, "Where are you from and what do you say about yourself? I have toiled in fighting for you and I could not save you. If you are the king of the Jews, say so with confidence."

Jesus answered and said to Pilate: "Do you say this of yourself, or have others told you about me?" Pilate said to him: "Am I a Jew, am I? Your people have delivered you to me. What have you done?"

Jesus answered: "My kingdom is not of this world. If my kingdom were of this world, my servants would fight so that no one deliver me to the Jews. Now my kingdom is not of this world."

Pilate said to him: "So, you are a king?"

Jesus answered: "You have said it: I am a king."

Pilate said to him, "If you are a king, teach me the truth from your mouth so that these troubles and revolutions may be far from you."

He then said to him: "Here you confess and say with your mouth that I am a king. I was born and came into the world for this purpose: to bear witness to the truth. Whoever is of me listens to my voice."

Pilate said to him, "What is truth?"

Jesus said to him: "Have you not seen that he who speaks with you is truth? Do you not see on his face that he was born of the Father? Do you not hear from the words of his mouth that he does not come from this world?
Know then, O Pilate, that he whom you judge, he will judge the world with justice. These hands that you seize, O Pilate, have formed (or created) you. This body that you see and this flesh that they have

11th FRAGMENT.

"(I afflicted myself) greatly because there is nothing that I can place in parallel with this other thing in a way that would make me say: 'My soul is sad unto death.'"

Similarly, I saw (by prophecy) the multitude of my compatriots surrounding me and chasing me with contempt; shouting against me; preparing a glass of vinegar and placing it before me; others preparing nails; others weaving a crown of thorns; the spear bearers surrounding me with their weapons... all this multitude of Jews shouting: "Take him! Take him! Crucify him!"

When I saw these things in this way, I afflicted myself greatly and unto death, seeing those whom I had created beautifully wanting to lose me wickedly in their folly; seeing the clay struggling against the potter; seeing the creature wanting to kill the one who created it; seeing the work of my hands while I stood before it as accused. I have not sinned and they did not find any malice in my mouth. That is why my soul was afflicted unto death."

After all these things, Pilate received the apologies of Jesus, saying (again): "If you are the king of the Jews, tell us with confidence."

Jesus said to him: "After all this time, do you still not know that I am the king, and that I am the one who formed you with my hands, O Pilate? It is my Father who sent me here so that I may bring man back to his original state, because since the time he violated our commandments, we have expelled him from Paradise due to his disobedience. Now I want to bring him back there again. Since Cain killed his brother Abel, the blood of the latter has not ceased to cry out until this hour. It will not cease to cry out until mine cries and his is silenced.
They have sawn Isaiah in two. They have quartered Jeremiah. They have strangled some. They have stoned others. They have struck a multitude of prophets, and to this day they have not ceased their audacity and impudence. They have killed the priest Zachariah, son of Barachiah, and John his son. And now they are attacking the one who is greater than all of them, that is to say, me."

When Pilate heard these words, he was very afraid. He brought Jesus into the midst of the Sanhedrin and said, "Here is the man you are looking for in this place." Then they cried out to Pilate, "Take him! Take him! Crucify him!" Pilate said to them [...]

12th FRAGMENT

[...] patient for them; for he is patient, knowing that they will come into his hands for judgment. Now there was a man from the crowd whose name was Ananias and who was from Bethlehem, the city of David. He rushed to the cross of Jesus, ran to him, placed his hands on the hands of the Son of God. He applied his heart to the heart of the Son of God. He kissed the feet of Jesus. He kissed the hands of Jesus. He kissed the mouth of Jesus. He kissed the side of Jesus that was pierced for our salvation.

He kissed all the members of the Son of God, saying, "O lying and impure Jews! Kill me, but do not kill the Son of God (stone me, but do not stone the Son of God. Crucify me, but do not crucify the Son of God), for Jesus is my Lord, Jesus is my God. He is the Christ."

When he had said these things, a voice came from the body of the Savior on the cross, saying, "Ananias, Ananias, your soul will not go to the Amenti, your body will not have the smell of the dead. Death will have no power over your body. Your name will be written on the gate of heaven and you will be called in heaven 'the firstfruits of immortality (or of blessing)."

These are the things that the body of the Son of God said, suspended on the cross.

The high priests were completely beside themselves, throwing stones at the man. The blessed elder Ananias opened his mouth to praise God, saying: "My heart rejoices in the sweet fragrance of the Son of God. The light of the Son of God has illuminated my soul and my body. I am full of joy. Glory to the Father and to the Holy Spirit forever! Amen."

The priests, after failing to stone the man to death, ordered him to be burned alive. When they lit the fiery blaze, the fire cooled his body, like a dewy wind. He remained in the midst of the fire for three days and three nights until the Savior resurrected from the dead. When they saw that the fire did not touch him, the high priests pierced him with a lance [...]"

At that moment, the Savior took Ananias' soul up with him to the heavens. The Lord said to him: "You are blessed, Ananias, because you believed in the Son of God while you were in the world. Not only did you believe..."

13th FRAGMENT

[...] "and all my members for you to examine. I am not ashamed indeed of the wounds that are in my body, I am not ashamed of the blows I have received, I will not hide the trophies of my victory and my glory; but I will manifest them and make them evident. The sun knows these things because it has darkened. The earth knows these things because it has been agitated, seeking a resting place for itself. The stones know these things because they have split, mourning my suffering by breaking themselves. The dead have known these things because of this they have risen and have come out of their tomb. The veil of the temple has known these things, for it has split and thus mourned first for the loss of the Jews. You see my hands as you wanted; you can penetrate my wounds with your fingers; if you want to see my side I will not afflict you (in this)."

"Here I reveal it to you. Bring your hand that seeks and wants to learn. Put your hand in my side and touch my body conceived without intervention of man. Touch my body that I received from the holy Virgin. Touch my body that is your relative. Touch my body that endured suffering according to my will. Touch my body that has died (and risen)."

14th FRAGMENT

The mothers in these lands who have seen the death of their sons, when they go to the tomb to see the bodies of those they mourn, a great comfort and [...] result for them. I went out to see him [...] above all these... raised on his cross like a thief [...] Here [...].

She opened her eyes, for they had been lowered so as not to look upon the earth because of the scandals. She said to him with joy: "Master, my lord, my God, my son, you have risen, truly risen." She wanted to seize him to kiss him on the mouth. But he prevented her and asked her, saying: "My mother, do not touch me. Wait a little, (for) it is the garment my Father has given me when. He has raised me. It is not possible that nothing carnal should touch me until I go to heaven. This body is, however, the one with which I spent nine months in your womb [...]. Know these things, oh my mother. This flesh is the one I received from you. That is the one that rested in my tomb. That is also the one that has been resurrected today, the one standing before you. Look at my hands and my feet. Oh Mary, my mother, know that it is me whom you have nourished. Do not doubt, oh my mother, that I am not your son. It is I who left you in the care of John when I was raised on the cross."

"Now then, oh my mother, hurry to warn my brothers and tell them [...] According to the words that I have spoken to you, go to Galilee: you will see me. Hurry, for it is not possible for me not to go to heaven to my Father, and not see you again."

15th FRAGMENT

"Those who have suffered with me on earth [...] More than all of these. Teach me how many Apostles took the body of Jesus in the tomb?"

He said, "They all came, the eleven, along with their disciples. They took it secretly and separated only from the other (Judas)."

He called the third and said to him, "I value your testimony more than many. Who took the body of Jesus in the tomb?"

He said, "Joseph with Nicodemus and their relatives."

He called the fourth. He said to him, "You are the most significant among them and I have sent them all away. Now tell me what happened when they took the body of Jesus from your hands in the tomb."

He said, "Our Lord, the praeses, behold, we were asleep. We forgot and could not know who took it. Then we woke up, searched for it, but did not find it [...] We warned [...]"

Pilate said to the Jews and the centurions, "These people lie in this way. Their words are divided (and contradict) for the lie! And he ordered that the soldiers be secured until he came to the tomb."

At that moment he rose with the Jewish elders and the Sanhedrin and the chief priests. They found the shrouds placed on the ground with no one there. Pilate said: "O men! Who hate your own life, if they had taken the body, (they would have taken) the strips as well."

They said to him: "Do you not see that these are not his, but others' foreign ones?"

Pilate remembered the words of Jesus: "Great miracles must take place in my tomb." So Pilate hurried to enter the tomb. He took Jesus's shrouds. He held them against his chest. He wept over them. He kissed them joyfully as if Jesus were surrounded by them.

He focused on the centurion standing at the tomb's door and saw that he had only one eye (for the other eye had been pierced in battle) and that he covered it with his hand all the time, not to see the light. Pilate [...] (Do you think that God will not) seek vengeance for the Lord's life? But the flame of his anger has come upon you."

They gave their consent to this condemnation by saying: "His blood be on us and on our children!"

Pilate said to the centurion: "My brother, do not give up the true life you have received, and that in vain for the sake of lies and the peace of the Jews."

This is what he said in the presence of the Jews (and the disciples of Christ). Pilate and the centurion were led to the well in the garden, a very deep well. I, Gamaliel, also followed them in the midst of the crowd. They looked down into the well.

The Jews cried out: "Oh Pilate, behold... Is this not the body of Jesus who has died?"

They (the disciples) said: "Our Lord, the shrouds that are on you are those of Jesus. This body is that of the thief who was crucified with Jesus [...] Joseph and Nicodemus (placed on the body) the bandages (that you have in your hands)."

Pilate remembered what Jesus had said: "The dead will rise in my tomb."

That is why he called the elders of the Jews and said to them: "Do you believe that he is the Nazarene?"

They said: "We believe it."

He said: "It is fitting to place his body in his tomb as is done for all the dead."

16th FRAGMENT

When he saw these apostles, he got up. He called them. He said, "Have mercy on my misery."

He turned to Peter and said to him: "I beg you, have mercy on me. Remember the moment when the servant girl talked to you, saying, 'You are a disciple of Jesus.' I rebuked her. So now, my father Peter, do not let me die in this torment."

Peter said to him: "This power does not belong to us; but if you believe in God and in his only son, Jesus Christ whom the Virgin bore, (you will obtain grace)."

This high priest replied: "We also know that he is the son of God. But what will you do about the greed that has blinded our eyes?"

And that with our fathers, (who), as they approached death, told us: "Behold, we have been made priests to serve at the head of the people and receive the firstfruits and tithes from their hands. But beware of loving money, lest God be angry with you. Give away what is extra to the poor and those in need. We did not obey the instructions of our fathers, but we became merchants buying and selling. Jesus came. He drove us out of the temple, saying: 'Do not let these people stay in this place; for they have turned my Father's temple into a market.' So we became angry because of his words, we made a plan together, we took him, we crucified him without knowing that he is the Son of God. Now, my father Peter, do not hold me accountable for my lack of faith. Forgive me for my audacity; behold, God did not want me to be blinded like the others who were not worthy to see the glory of the body of my Lord's mother."

Then Peter said to him: "If you believe in Christ, go embrace the body of the Virgin by saying: 'I believe in you and in the one you have borne, a virgin without.'

Speaking in Hebrew, blessing God and testifying to what is written in the law and the prophets about Christ, so that the apostles marveled at everything he said.

He then took his severed hand, applied it to its place, saying, "In the name of the one who was crucified on the cross, the one whom the Virgin Mary bore, Jesus Christ, you will also listen to me today, you will receive my prayer, and you will make my arm adhere back in its place; for I, my Lord, saw you reattach the servant of the high priest's ear that Peter had cut off."

As soon as he stopped speaking, his hand adhered as before. Peter said to him, "Rise, take palm branches from this palm tree and go to the city: You will find there multitudes of blind men; you will tell them all that has happened to you. Whoever believes in Christ, put these palm branches on his eyes and he will see; whoever does not believe in him will not see."

The high priest found a multitude of blind men sitting, crying out, "Woe to us! What happened to the people of Sodom has happened to us."

At that moment, the high priest spoke with them about Christ and what had happened to him. All those who erred saw. However, the apostles carried the body of the Virgin. They placed it in the tomb. They remained in that place waiting for the Lord to resurrect the body of the Virgin from the dead and take her to heaven with him, as he had said. The apostles said to the virgins who followed them, "Each of you should return to your home in peace."

The virgins did not want to, because they also desired to stay in that place.

Peter and John told them, "Be brave, my daughters. Go in peace. Christ will guide you. We have safely placed his body (of the Virgin) because it was the dwelling place of the Word of the Father. Do not make us like a wedding procession, by staying between us and our Master, for the Jews hate him. Now we have placed his body (of the Virgin) in the tomb. But we believe that he will not leave it forever. He will come to resurrect it as he told us. I tell you this: Your sorrow will not fall, for you serve the Mother of the Lord."

They told them these things, consoling them. They said, "Blessed are you, our fathers, so that this blessing may be with us in our places of residence."

Peter said to John: "Rise, my brother, bless them."

John said to him: "Forgive me, my lord and father, to you belongs the glory."

Peter made them bow their heads. He blessed them saying: "I pray to you, Lord Jesus Christ, true shepherd, who gathers his sheep and does not leave the man lost in the hand of the devil, for you have saved him with your holy blood; Jesus our Lord, Jesus our strength, Jesus our hope, Jesus our life, Jesus our joy; you will bless us, you will shade us with the shadow of your wings. Glory to you and to your good Father, to the Holy Spirit, forever! Amen."

When he had said these things, behold, the man who believed in God came to the tomb at the third hour of the day. He found the apostles sitting. He said to them: "Where is my father Peter?"

They called him and he came in haste. The high priest said to him, "Forgive me, my father, that I may tell you all the things that have happened to me- So when I came to the city, I told them what had happened to me. When the Jews heard this, they were filled with anger against you because of Mary, the mother of the Lord. They spoke together, saying, "What shall we do? For when Jesus, his Son, was crucified, we said, 'The disciples secretly took him away at night.' Now that his mother has died, we went to burn her body, but we could only find her resting place. We set it on fire, but it did not burn."

And they said, "They must have placed her in the tomb. Let us now burn her and her tomb so that she cannot be found at all, lest she rise again like her Son, and the final error be worse than the first."

Others said, "We are blind and cannot see."

Finally, they agreed on a plan: "Let us burn her this time."

So when I learned of their plan, I came to warn you of all that has happened. Go! Hide yourselves, lest they come and find you and kill you. After saying these things, he went to his house in great secrecy. Peter warned the disciples. But God caused the high priests to forget. They did not search for the Virgin's body again saying, "We escaped the first time we wanted to go there. Let's stay."

Peter and John gained confidence. They left the place to God. They stayed together saying, "Let's not leave the body. She has the strength to pray for us and save us."

They were still gathered talking about the greatness of God. Then a voice came to them, saying, "Do not fear, my chosen ones, nothing bad will happen to you. These atheists will not come back to you. Stay. I will resurrect her body (the Virgin's) without delay. I will shame these impious Jews."

When the voice had said these things, it returned to the heavens in glory. After that, we reached the sixteenth hour; we spoke thus, gathered with the apostles recounting the great miracles of God. We saw flashes above us at the door of the tomb where the Virgin was; we were very afraid. After that, a loud noise was heard, so we said to ourselves: The tomb will collapse on us, and we smelled a good odor spreading. Then there were loud voices and flashes of light and fire. We saw the Lord Jesus extending his right hand. He embraced us. He gave us peace. After that, he called my mother, Mary, my bond of rest in which I have been, to rise; leave behind these shrouds and come out of the tomb.

"As my Father raised me from the dead, I will raise you to take you to heaven with me." We looked; then we saw the Holy Virgin Mary carrying the garment (the body) in which she had been born, as if she had not seen death at all. We saw the Lord Jesus extending his hand, lifting her onto the chariot of light that carried him. We saw choirs of angels walking before them until they reached the heavens. We were still amazed as we looked behind us when we heard a voice saying: "Peace be with you, my brothers, do not fear; no harm will come to you."

Indeed, the miracle that occurred on that day, when the Virgin was raised from the dead, is greater than when the Lord was raised from the dead. The day when the Lord was raised from the dead, we did not see it, but only Mary, his mother, and Mary Magdalene: they are the ones to whom he appeared. They came, they warned us. We went to the tomb, we did not find his body, but only his burial clothes that we found and that were laid there. We did not see him until we arrived in Galilee where we found him. When he was raised from the dead, we saw flashes of light and heard trumpets, we saw [...]

In this way, the Virgin was taken up to heaven [...]

We, the apostles, can testify to these things. We have not added anything to it; we have not taken away anything from what we have seen with our own eyes, from what we have heard from the mouth of Our Lord Jesus Christ, the Word who became flesh like all men and who is now at the right hand of the Father. And the flesh in which the Virgin was conceived in her mother's womb, she herself is resurrected, she is at the right hand of her Son Jesus Christ. She prays for the whole world and the Father receives the supplications and prayers that she makes for us more than those of all the saints.
At the time when God will judge all humanity, everyone will see Him (Christ) bearing the flesh that he received from the holy Virgin Mary. After these things, we went to the tomb. We found the clothes deposited in the place where his body had been placed: we buried them [...] We [...]

The Scriptorium Project is the work of a small group of lay people of various apostolic churches who are interested in the preservation, transmission, and translation of the works of the early and medieval church. Our efforts are to make the works of the church fathers accessible to anyone who might have an interest in Christian antiquities and the theological, philosophical, and moral writings that have become the bedrock of Western Civilization.

To-date, our releases have pulled from the Greek, Syriac, Georgian, Latin, Celtic, Ethiopian, and Coptic traditions of Christianity, and have been pulled from sundry local traditions and languages.

www.ingramcontent.com/pod-product-compliance
Lightning Source LLC
LaVergne TN
LVHW052049070526
838201LV00086B/5156